UPROOTED

Published by Context, an imprint of Westland Books, a division of Nasadiya Technologies Private Limited, in 2025

No. 269/2B, First Floor, 'Irai Arul', Vimalraj Street, Nethaji Nagar, Alapakkam Main Road, Maduravoyal, Chennai 600095

ISBN: 9789360455545

10 9 8 7 6 5 4 3 2 1

Design and Layout by Nishant Kumar

Printed at Thomson Press (India) Ltd

UPROOTED

A GRAPHIC ACCOUNT OF THE STRUGGLE FOR FOREST RIGHTS

ITA MEHROTRA

FOREWORD BY **AMEER HAMZA**
& INTROUCTION BY **ORIJIT SEN**

Foreword

Ameer Hamza

My name is Ameer Hamza, and I am the founder of Van Gujjar Tribal Yuva Sangathan (VGTYS), located in Haridwar District, Uttarakhand. The Van Gujjar community is semi-nomadic and we go on seasonal migrations with our buffaloes, both to the high-altitude meadows in Uttarakhand as well as in the plains. Over the years, the establishment of national parks in Uttarakhand has severely affected our forest-dwelling lifestyle and our migratory routes uphill. Many families from our community have been either forced to give up on migrating with their animals altogether, or they attempt to go towards other areas in Uttar Pradesh, like the wetland 'khaadar' between Bijnour and Muzaffarnagar.

The VGTYS has worked tirelessly to secure our community's rights to access and manage the forests that we have lived in for many generations. Another key focus area for us is the education and skills development of our younger generation, in a manner that is linked to the life of the Van Gujjars. We have been running schools in the remote forest locations that our community lives in, and working towards methods of learning that include both our traditional knowledge systems as also regular school curriculum.

We have seen how children and young people are powerfully moved by image-based books, and how this encourages them towards learning. We, therefore, believe that *Uprooted*, bringing our stories and struggles on to the pages of a book through drawings, maps and words, is a powerful tool for our work within and also outside of our communities. This book brings to light not only our everyday life and traditions, but also the many urgent conversations and initiatives that the younger members of the community are taking up. We feel it is a useful and important method of also reaching other young people, to share with them our ongoing struggles from inside the forest and resettlement colonies.

Today, we Van Gujjars in Uttarakhand find ourselves caught between development projects that don't benefit forest-dwelling communities and the growing communal tensions that are increasingly threatening us. We are often needlessly stopped by police and vigilante groups in the hill towns we cross on our migratory routes. Our ability to be economically secure and rely on the sale of our buffalo milk to nearby towns and cities is also being severely threatened. In the midst of these growing struggles, I strongly believe that it is all the more urgent that we are able to strengthen our organisation, and to share the work we do with a wider public. I hope that *Uprooted* will be one step in that direction.

Ameer Hamza is the founder of the Van Gujjar Yuva Tribal Sangathan. He lives and works in Kunao Chaur, Haridwar District, Uttarakhand.

Introduction

Orijit Sen

Uprooted is a sensitive portrayal of a forest-based pastoral community caught up in the snares of development and change. The historical process of the appropriation, re-shaping and re-management of natural commons and resources by the State have been disastrous for itinerant communities everywhere in the world, and the story of the Van Gujjars is no different. Although told through the voices of living members of the community, the historical, even 'civilisational', forces behind their disenfranchisement is never far in the background of Ita Mehrotra's long-form comics documentary.

Ita follows individuals and groups of Van Gujjars in different settlements around and within the Rajaji National Park – conversing, observing, listening, drawing and writing. Their discussions range from forests and gathering, animals, food, community life, artisanal work, education of children, jobs for the new generation and many other concerns. But at the core of all these diverse conversations is the central question of the Van Gujjar way of life, the manifold threats it faces today, and what the future holds for them as a community. Most of the Van Gujjar characters we meet in Ita's episodic and well-structured narration are not just resilient and strong in their own ways; they also have a remarkable and politically astute understanding of how Indian forest policies and the commodification of their habitats are disempowering them and alienating them from their very identity. And they are fighting back as best as they can.

I am reminded of the similar agitations that grew into the now well-known Chipko Andolan in the Garhwal forests in the 1970s. Will the Van Gujjars also be able to collectively and radically resist the onslaught of the exploitative government–corporate nexus at work today? The stories that Ita narrates allow their courage, defiance and determination to shine through amidst the deepening sense of darkness. What started during the colonial era with the introduction of British Forest Laws, continues today more than 150 years on, like a genocide in slow motion. Some younger generation activists have collectivised the resistance – forming groups such as the Van Gujjar Tribal Yuva Sangathan – and are working to monitor the unfair and insensitive resettlement programmes introduced, in essence, to drive out Van Gujjar communities from the forest areas and force them to adopt a settled, agricultural way of life. Such programmes are being pushed by the government regardless of the fact that agriculture is something the Van Gujjars have never practised and have no traditional knowledge or experience of. What they do have is a deep knowledge of forest resources and how to manage them in a sustainable way. It is not a surprise then that the Forest Department – which is mandated to do exactly that – wants to drive Van Gujjars out. For them, forest conservation for commercial exploitation is the underlying priority. Ita makes an insightful observation when she reflects at one point that the relationship between nature and human settlements is maintained by those who go between the two with their animals: the pastoral people.

Ita's work documents the complexities of the situation in great visual detail, weaving a richly layered narrative in the best non-fiction comics tradition. Her depictions of the characters, landscapes, forests, trees, Van Gujjar houses, animals, objects and material culture are precise and wonderfully detailed, adding greatly not only to the information conveyed, but also to the emotive quality of the experience that the book offers. Doing this in black and white is challenging for an artist, and her delicate line and wash technique do the job admirably.

Prologue

In the summer of 2024, as temperatures soared to over forty-five degrees, forest fires raged through the foothills of Uttarakhand.
Dassowali Gujjarkhata, Haridwar District
The homes of several Van Gujjar families who live in these forests were burnt to ashes. Also gone were their documents, belongings, buffaloes, goats and fodder collected over the years.
The police visited, declared that the fire was caused by an earthen stove left unattended, and then they went away.

Even as they grappled with all that had been lost, it was members of the community themselves, organised by their own youth leaders, who rallied together to arrange food, shelter and fodder for families that had been left homeless.

After all, it wasn't the first time the Van Gujjars had dealt with the absolute apathy of the state, or the results of forced ecological imbalances growing around them ...

1. In the Time of Trees

I built this home with my own hands.
So that my three children and I have a roof over our heads.
Dried palm leaves, dead branches from the forest. And earth packed in.

On warmer summer nights, we sleep in the room with no walls.
Come, let's go inside.

Van Gujjar Dera, Asarori Range,
Rajaji National Park, Uttarakhand

We are in Noorjahan's home at the edge of Dehradun, where the fast-expanding city finally recedes and the old forests, those that still remain, begin.
Having worked as a lawyer and activist here, my friend Zuha knows the Van Gujjar community well.

I built this house two years ago.
My brothers and father helped me.
We have what we need here.
And I feel peaceful amongst the trees.

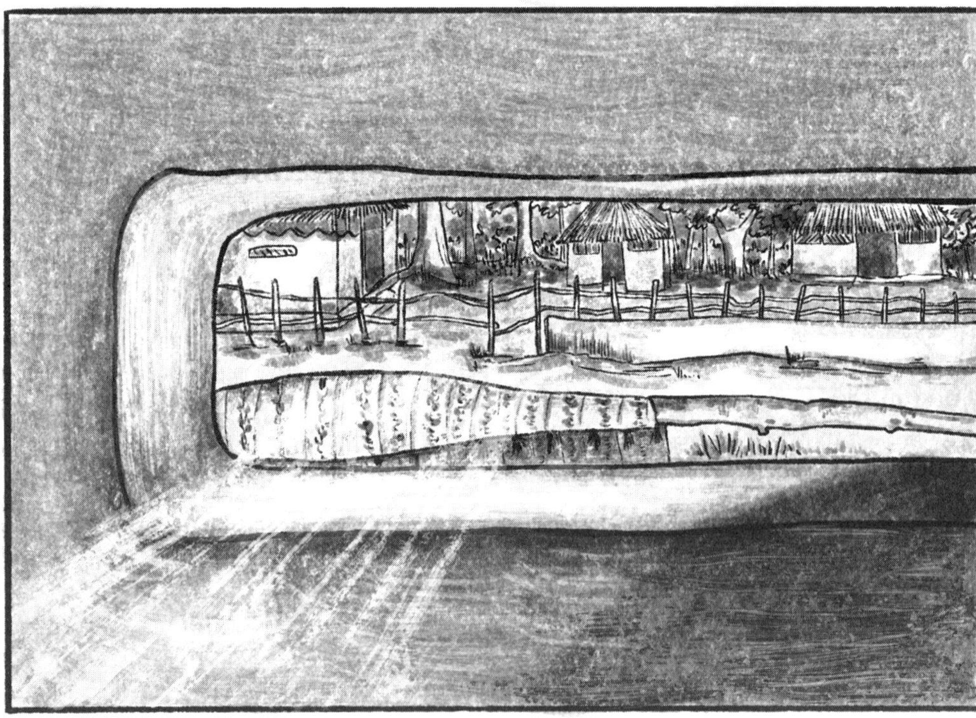

It turns out that sparrows and other small birds here have dedicated nesting spaces between the beams and thatch. Noorjahan's home, like that of most forest-dwelling Van Gujjars, is not crafted for humans alone.

Noorjahan says she doesn't like feeling cooped in and wants to see trees from inside her home. This is clear from the many large windows she has built in, each a different shape.

But if you really want to know how we continue to live here, you have to understand the threat that hangs over our heads, day after day ...
Wild animals and forest fires don't scare us. We know very well how to deal with all that.
What is scary is the threat of the Junglaat and sarkar.

It is because of that constant pressure, that so many families have left from this forest in the past twenty-five years.
You can't even imagine how big this Dera used to be earlier.
And when there were more of us here, the forests were actually thicker and larger ...

We used to have thousands of buffaloes!
We still do, but far fewer. Back then, we had more animals than you could count. There were cows, hens and goats too, but the Gojri buffalo has always been our whole life!
And they love to walk ...
At the start of spring, we would walk uphill with the animals. We trekked for weeks untill we reached the high pastures of Garhwal.
Earlier, we used to walk on narrow paths. Then the highways came so we began to stay on the roadsides, wherever we could.
The whole family used to travel up.
A few of us still go up.

The pastures in the mountains are the most beautiful places on earth. But even in beautiful places you have to work very hard, no?
Making sure the animals have fodder. That they don't get too cold. Then collecting milk and walking many miles to nearby towns to sell it every day.
Sankri, Uttarkashi District, Garhwal Himalayas

Many in my family still walk up to the pastures every year. They return as winter begins.
Before we leave, we take down the roofs of the huts we set up there, so that the snow doesn't settle on top of them. Otherwise they will all come crashing down.
So there's hardly anything we leave behind.

We could live in a pasture or forest for months.
But once we've gone, it's hard to tell we were there at all ...

But even up there, the Junglaat would not leave us alone!
They blame us Van Gujjars for cutting down forests that we actually help nourish! What better fertiliser is there than the dung of our buffaloes?
Why would we harm the forests when our whole life depends on them?
Ever since I was a child they have wanted us out of here. They say it is to protect the forest, the elephants, the tigers ...
Established in 1983, Rajaji National
encompasses the Shivaliks, at the
foothills of the Himalayas. It includes three
districts of Uttarakhand- Haridwar, Dehradun
and Pauri Garhwal. In 2015 Rajaji was
granted the prestigious status of being
notified as a tiger reserve, making it the
second tiger reserve in the state, after
Corbett. To mark this occasion the Chief
Minister released a brand new logo for RNP
and said it should be known not only for its
conservation efforts, wildlife and natural
but rather, it should utilize these to boost
tourism and financial sector of the state.
Spread across over 1075 sq.km. now,
48 TRs across India
made a TR in 1973-same year as Chipko movement(!)
(!!)
ANIMALS AT RAJAJI
BENGAL TIGER
ASIAN ELEPHANT
FANTA
LEOPARD
GORAL
STRIPED HYENA
BEAR
hello!
They keep building new fences, new boundaries, new rules.

For whom is this park? These forests were always ours and we belong to them. This is the only life we know, so why would we destroy it?
You won't believe it but even the deer and elephants like to keep close to our Dera. Why, in the hot summer months they come down and drink from the water channels that we make!
I've seen that happen so many times around sunset. The animals sense that we will not harm them.
And every living being has the same thirst to quench, no?
But who wants to listen to an illiterate woman like me? If the forest authorities cared about those living here at all, they would have left us alone during the lockdown ...

Without warning, a huge group of the Junglaat came and tried to break the roof and walls of my home. This was in the summer of 2020. It was anyways a difficult time because milk sales were so low.
When my father and others in my family tried to fight back, they beat us up. I remember that some of our clothes tore because they dragged me and other women out of our homes.
They dragged us by our hair.
And then they filed a case against us. But that's not the first time this has happened, and it won't be the last.

They think they own these forests. But they don't even know the forests!
If it was up to us, we would want to continue living within this forest. This is our home. We will protect it.
But this constant pressure makes me think of leaving ...
If you were allotted land by the government to resettle outside the forest, would you take it?
Look at the time! It's getting dark earlier, as winter comes.
There's one calf of mine that hasn't returned yet. I'll have to go find her.

Where is my daughter? She took the buffaloes uphill to graze today.
Haleema, has the calf come back or not? Look how dark it is already!
Usually, they come home by themselves. Today, they've decided to wander off ...

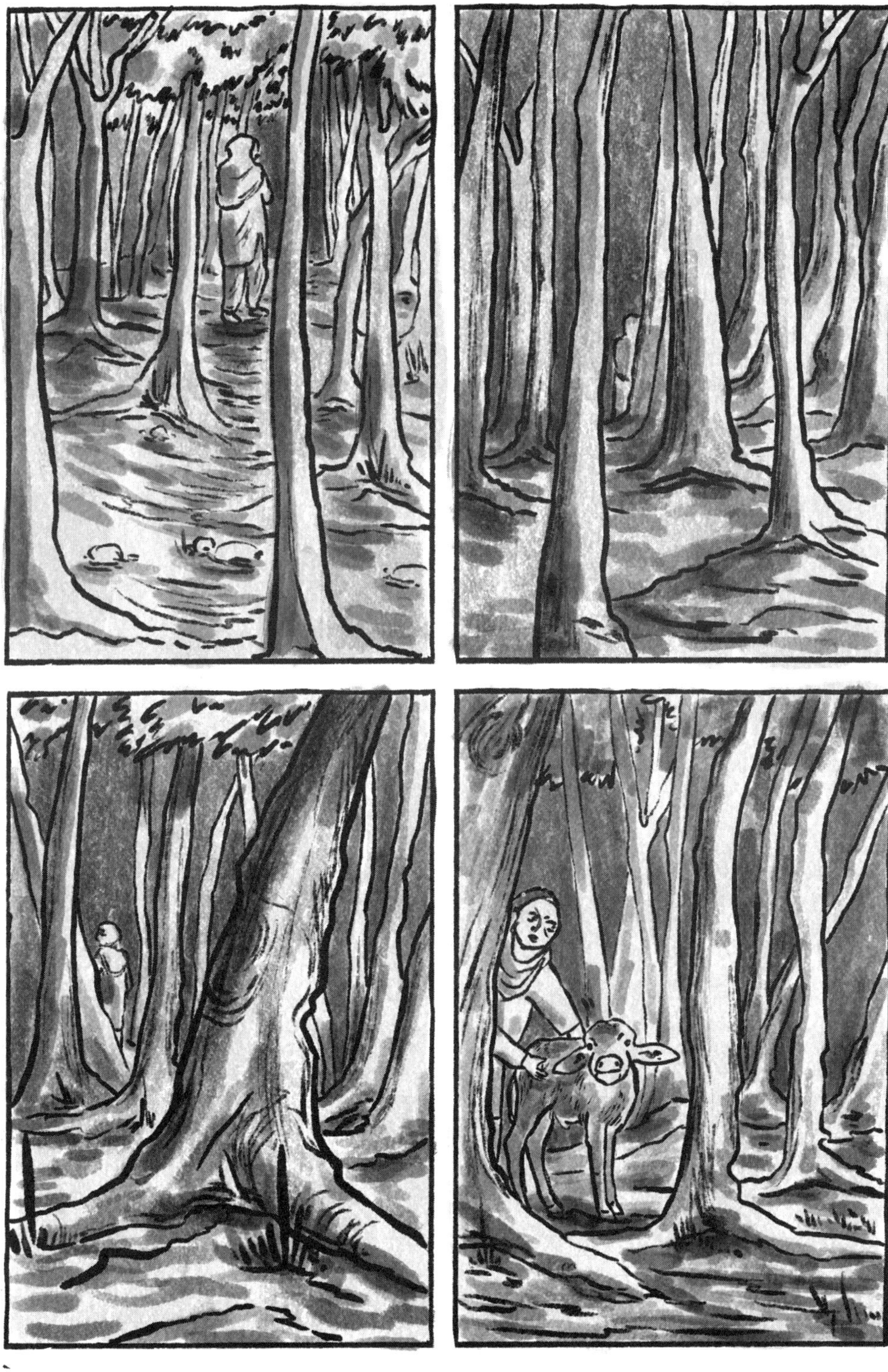

The highway adjacent to the Dera connects Delhi to Dehradun.
Massive construction is underway to convert it into a much wider expressway, so as to be able to bring multitudes of tourists as speedily as possible up to Uttarakhand's high-altitude Hindu sites of worship, the Char Dham, and to the many hotels perched on the edge of crumbling mountain sides. The enormous new highway bites its way right through the foothills and forests. But then, roads have always been good at doing that.

CHARDHAM YATRA
FIXED DEPARTURE
A PILGRIMAGE TO INNER PEACE
YAMUNOTRI, GANGOTRI, KEDARNATH AND BADRINATH
SPECIAL OFFER
Book Your Spiritual Journey
9816119815

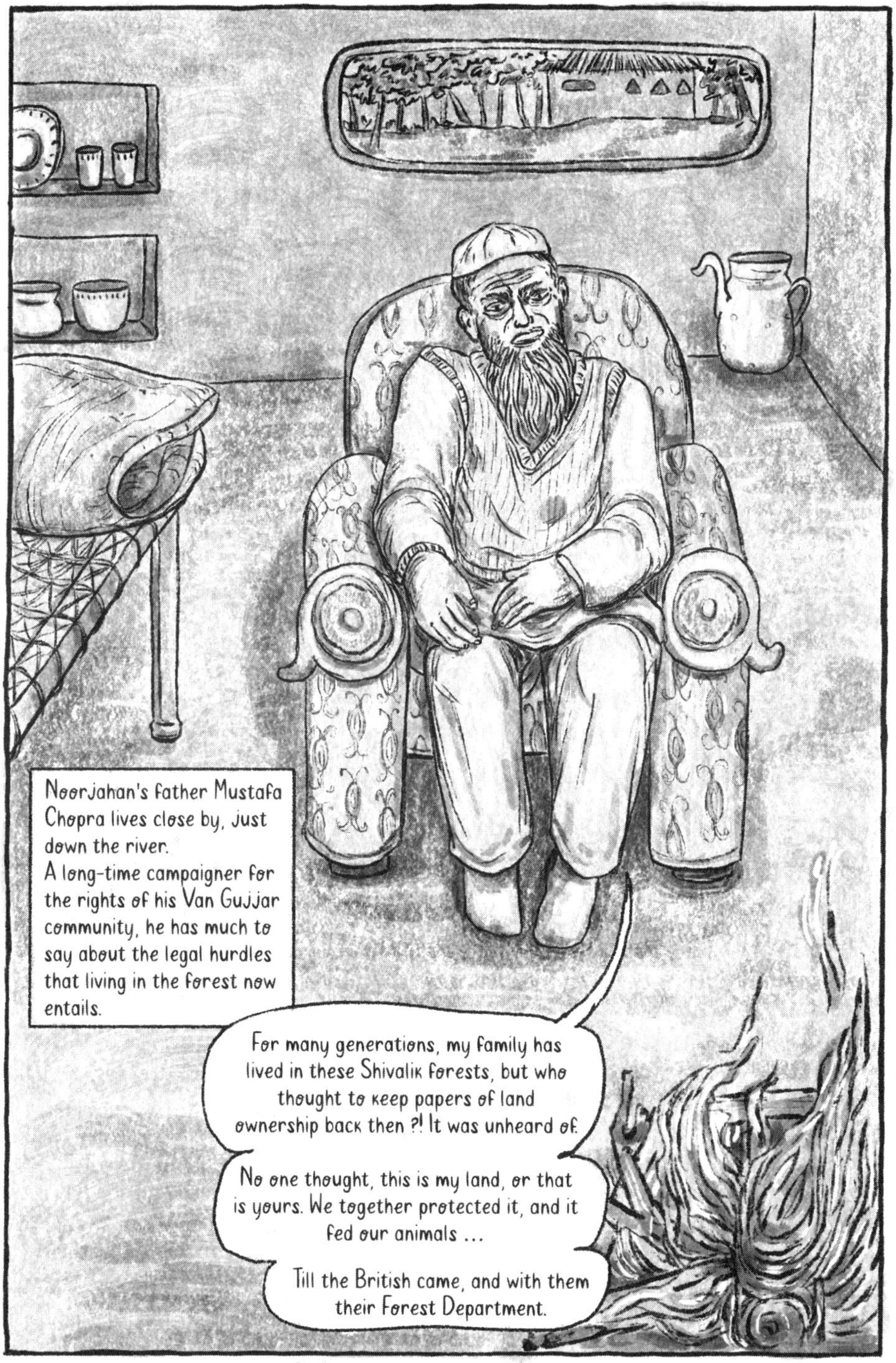

Noorjahan's father Mustafa Chopra lives close by, just down the river.
A long-time campaigner for the rights of his Van Gujjar community, he has much to say about the legal hurdles that living in the forest now entails.
For many generations, my family has lived in these Shivalik forests, but who thought to keep papers of land ownership back then ?! It was unheard of.
No one thought, this is my land, or that is yours. We together protected it, and it fed our animals ...
Till the British came, and with them their Forest Department.

During their rule, the British gave us grazing permits for small areas, here and on our migration routes. Even today, those permit reciepts are all we have to prove that we have been here for years ...
That we ARE here.
You have to go way back into history, and see how when in 1864 the Forest Department was established and colonial forest laws were imposed, they were meant to control the forest. To bring it under their rule. They claimed it was to protect the forests, but instead they looted them and converted that land into plantations.
Plantations are not forests, they are farms.
And the same mentaility continues even today. Governments come and go, and even though we have all our identification papers, we just don't exist!
It is only since 2006, with the Forest Rights Act, that we tribal and forest-dwelling communities have got some legal power to fight back with.

That Act was passed after many decades of struggle by adivasis and forest-dwellers like us, along with those who supported our rights.
According to it, if we can show that we have lived here for three generations, then we should have the legal title to this land within the forest.
For the FIRST time in history, there was a way for us to use the law!

Have you and your family filed a claim for this land under the FRA then?
Yes of course! We filed for Community Forest Rights, which is meant to recognise not just our land titles but also our rights to access the forests and forest produce, and to manage them. We filed in 2017.
Various activists helped us with filing for it, there are SO many documents, maps, identifications that need to be put together!!

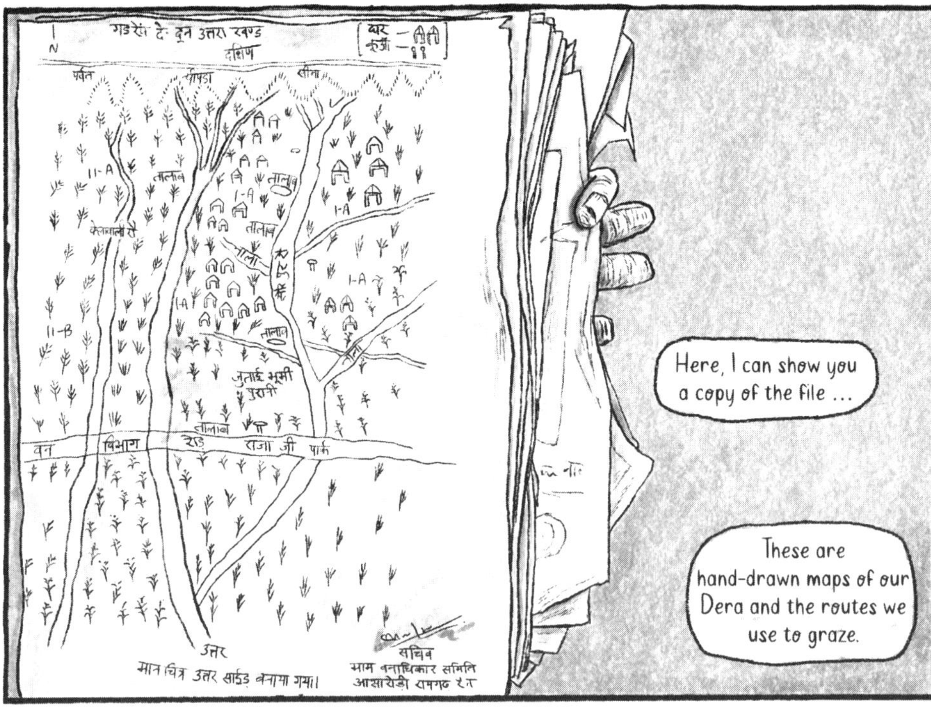
Here, I can show you a copy of the file ...
These are hand-drawn maps of our Dera and the routes we use to graze.

कब्रिस्तान, आशारोड़ी
यह कब्रिस्तान सदियों पुराना है।
We took photos of the old places, like graves that have been here for many generations.

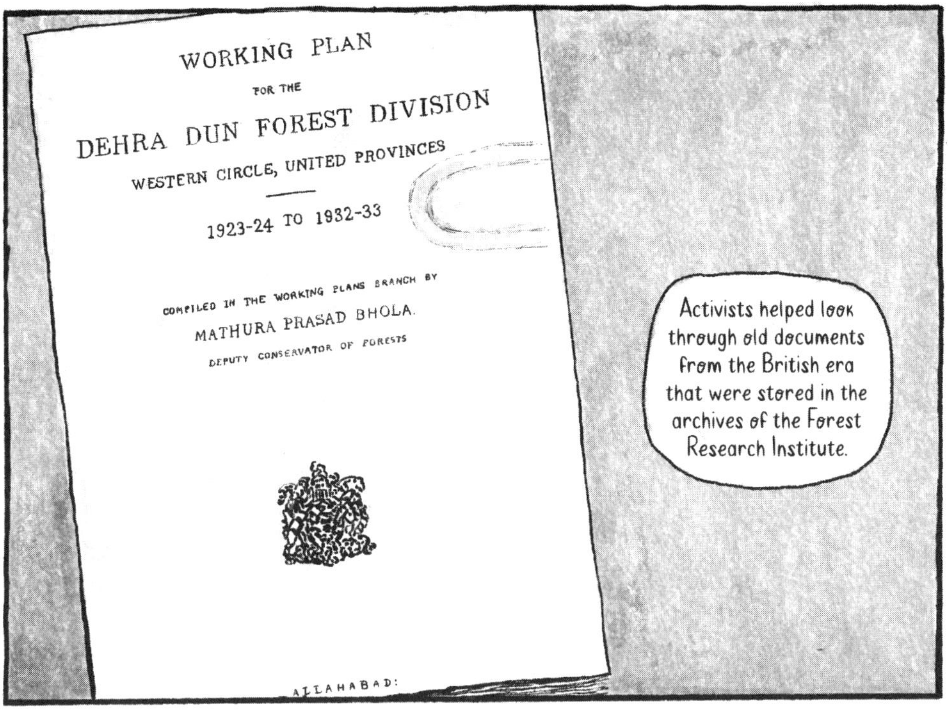
WORKING PLAN
FOR THE
DEHRA DUN FOREST DIVISION
WESTERN CIRCLE, UNITED PROVINCES
1923-24 TO 1932-33
COMPILED IN THE WORKING PLANS BRANCH BY
MATHURA PRASAD BHOLA.
DEPUTY CONSERVATOR OF FORESTS
ALLAHABAD:
Activists helped look through old documents from the British era that were stored in the archives of the Forest Research Institute.

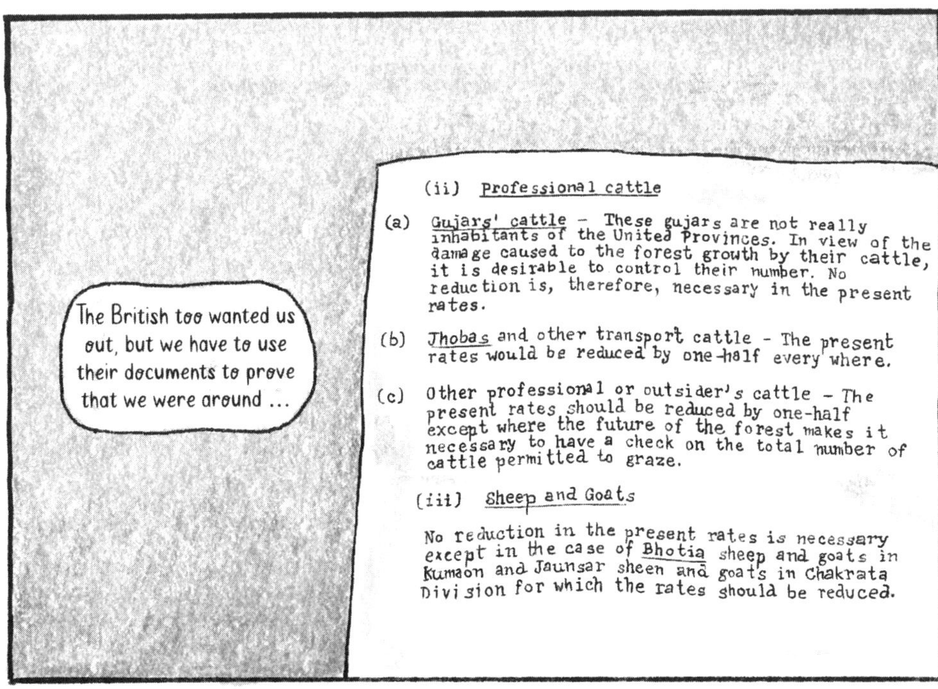
The British too wanted us out, but we have to use their documents to prove that we were around ...
(ii) Professional cattle
(a) Gujars' cattle - These gujars are not really inhabitants of the United Provinces. In view of the damage caused to the forest growth by their cattle, it is desirable to control their number. No reduction is, therefore, necessary in the present rates.
(b) Jhobas and other transport cattle - The present rates would be reduced by one-half every where.
(c) Other professional or outsider's cattle - The present rates should be reduced by one-half except where the future of the forest makes it necessary to have a check on the total number of cattle permitted to graze.
(iii) Sheep and Goats
No reduction in the present rates is necessary except in the case of Bhotia sheep and goats in Kumaon and Jaunsar sheep and goats in Chakrata Division for which the rates should be reduced.

Even though we put every document together carefully, no one knows when our claims will be met. Till date, barely any land titles have been given across the state!
Being a minority community in Uttarakhand without the Scheduled Tribe status makes our struggle even more challenging
As long as the application for CFR is pending, at least we can't legally be moved. But who will fight for all this after I am gone?

Meanwhile, I have my hands full with all the other false cases they keep filing against us. There are eight other cases against me! Including one for committing murder, can you believe it?? And one case against Noorjahan and her sons.
All of it is to slowly pressure us out, then they can make more roads, parks, airports.

We know that the forests and animals need our help to survive. The Department makes no effort to plant trees. All they do is promote tourism round the year. These days, even during the mating season.
All the trees you see here, lemon, guava, mango – we planted them.
For the birds, and for us.
Because we live right inside the forest, we can tell you better than anyone else what the Forest Department is up to. Even today their contractors come with trucks at night and cut away big old sal, eucalyptus and oak trees …
We see it all happening. But if we try to stop them, they will turn around and slap another case on us!

I follow Noorjahan's sister-in-law Ramzaan, as she and her daughters go into the valley on their daily walk to collect fodder, one afternoon.
We go further into what is the 'core zone' of the National Park.
You city people really don't know how to walk here!

See those marks? The elephants have been here just this morning. We should head back before it gets dark.

This one at the back, her name is Rosie. She's like the pack leader. They all have names so I can call out to them, but the pack goes where Rosie goes!

In the summers we even leave the buffaloes out at night, deep in the forest.
The tigers know them.
They have their own understanding of each other.

That one looks like it hasn't been cut in a few years!
We reach a clearing towards the top of the hills an hour or so away from the Dera.
As Ramzaan's daughter explains, they will lop off the branches only of specific trees.
We leave each tree for two years after lopping so it grows back fully.
See, when I cut these smaller branches the trunk will still stay strong ...
How do I draw how very high up she is?!

I've walked these routes all my life. You leave me here in the middle of the night and I'll find my way back.
We are the ones who make these footpaths! Just like you city folk, even the Junglaat people have no clue how to walk through the denser areas …
It's not just fodder for the animals we get here. In the warmer months it's full of berries.
Here, you should taste the wild fruit of our forests yourself.
AAMLA

This malwaar bel grows all over the area. We use it as a rope to tie our big bundles.
You want to carry this?? Hahaha!
As the sun sets, we make our way back to the Dera. Ramzaan and her daughters carry impossible loads carefully balanced with a stone placed between their heads and the malwaar rope. And I just about keep pace.

Once we are clear of elephant territory, we rest a while in the dry parts of the riverbed.

Of course I wanted to study and to send my children to school ...
But where is the school that we can go to? Why can't there be one in the forest when there are enough children who want to study?
Our children could then look after the animals and help us at home during the mornings, and then they could run along to study in the afternoons ...
Even if we manage to send them to the faraway government school, they don't understand Hindi when they are very young, so they just drop out. What's wrong with learning in our Gojri language?

Late evening, the children take me to the stream to fill water.
Next year, we are going to study.
Where?
They will bring a teacher here.
I saw you drawing my mother. Now draw me!
Do you miss going to school?
If we lived in Dehradun we would be studying. But then how would I walk in the forest?

2. The Resettlement

I am with Ameer Hamza and his colleague Aftab, of the Van Gujjar Tribal Yuva Sangathan.
We are travelling to one of the Resettlement Colonies near Haridwar.

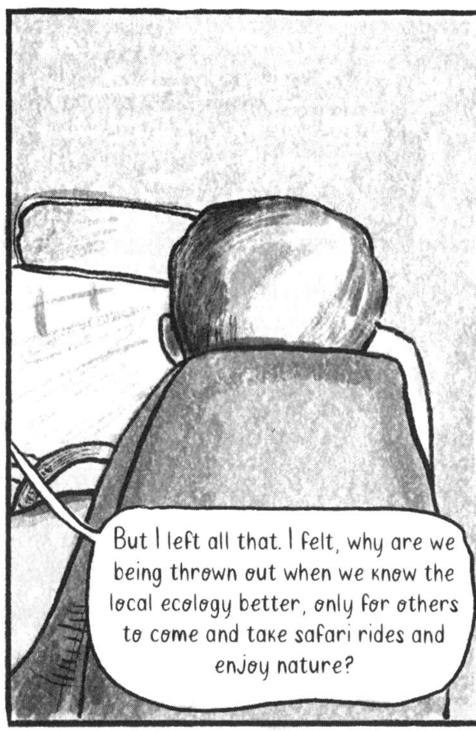

Earlier in the day, we had met at Ameer's Dera in the forests of Kunao Chaur. His Dera also falls within the forest area demarcated under the 'Chilla Range' of Rajaji National Park now.

The Uttarakhand government keeps coming up with welfare schemes for pastoral and tribal communities. They sound good, and yet no benefit really reaches us!
The thick mud walls kept us cool, even though the sun was blazing outside. Ameer spoke passionately about the MANY reasons for setting up the VGTYS.
During the lockdown, the government completely forgot about us. If we did not have the forest produce and our buffaloes, we wouldn't have survived.
There was NO schooling for our children when classes went online. We don't have electricity, hardly any smartphones and almost no network!
So we built our own schools. Our educated members, like Aftab, started teaching the children, using examples from our forest life – maths is taught through milk sales!

If you map the forest areas where Van Gujjar Deras are, you'll see that they get hit less by forest fires that burn down entire hillsides each year!
We clear dry branches, plant trees that are indigenous to this area, and we are much faster at controlling fires than the corrupt Forest Department...
54,000 hectares of forest cover affected by wild fires
Uttarakhand - March 2023
There were 21,847 cases of forest fires in the state in 2020-21. There is a direct correlation between the frequency of forest fires and climate cha

So while the main aim is to form a strong network across Uttarakhand to fight for our community's claims under the Forest Rights Act, with the hope of one day being recognised as legal owners of this land, we also take on so much more ...
See the tree cover around here? We have carefully protected it over generations. And when we meet the Forest officials, I end up explaining the legalities of FRA to THEM! District officials seem completely unaware that we have rights too or that such a law even EXISTS!

As we carry on towards the Resettlement Colony, Ameer talks about the interconnected struggles of livelihoods, land and ecology in his forest village.
At some point, the road ends in a river bed.

People from the cities are going to start running towards our villages and forests!
But we need the land to be legally ours, or else they will destroy these areas also! And then they will build resorts ...

We pass through towns where it is hard to tell the difference between hotels, temples and shops.
GANGA VIEW No1
RAM HALWAI
SRÎ BABA HOTEL
CRYING CREAM
And where traffic is regulated only by religious processions.
There's always some festival or pooja going on. We have to be more and more careful nowadays ...

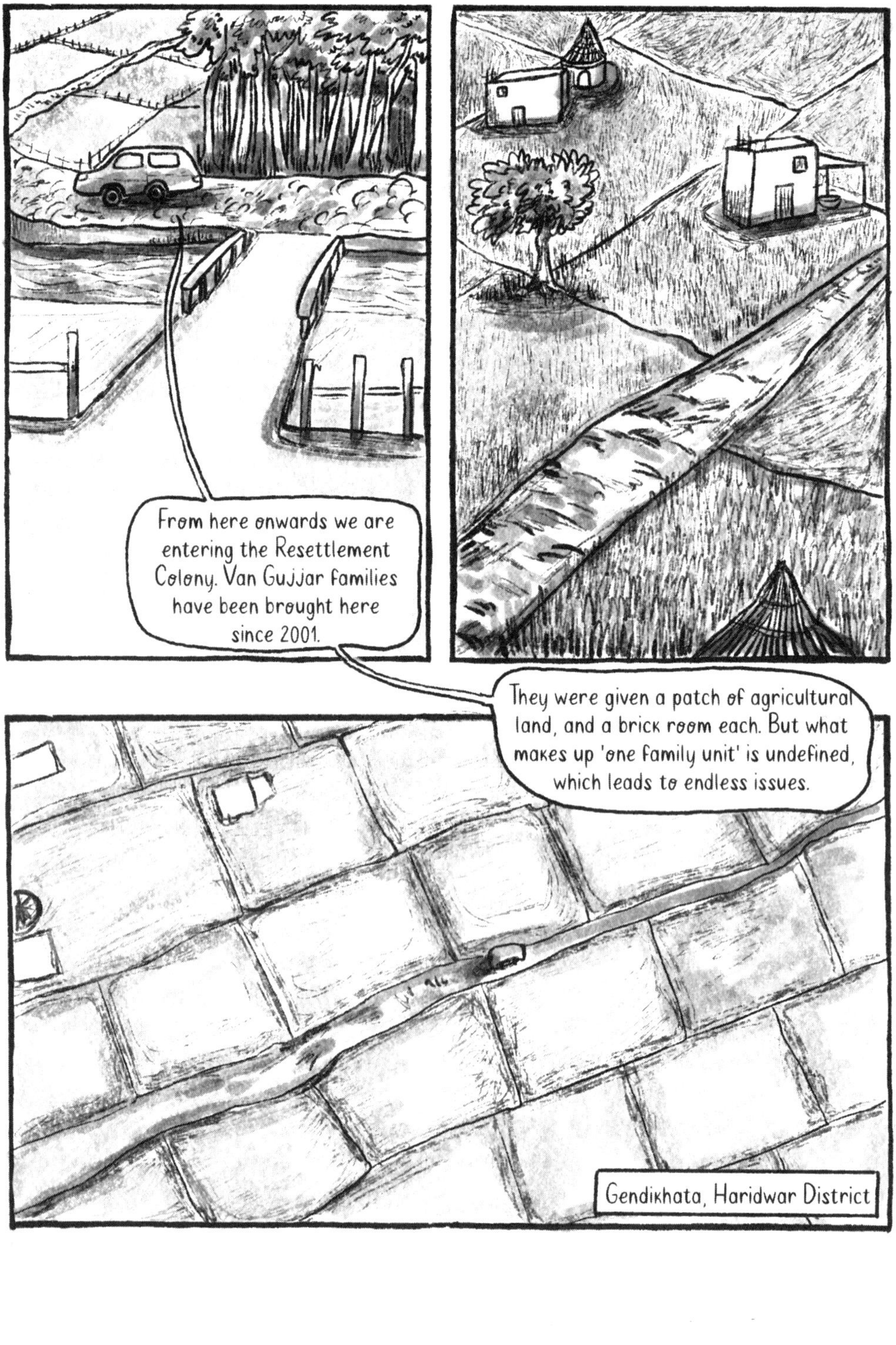
From here onwards we are entering the Resettlement Colony. Van Gujjar families have been brought here since 2001.
They were given a patch of agricultural land, and a brick room each. But what makes up 'one family unit' is undefined, which leads to endless issues.
Gendikhata, Haridwar District

And what happens when families expand? How do they live off this same tiny piece of land?
Most of them had left their cattle behind. They'd sold them or just let them loose. But once they realised there was no way to earn a living here, they bought one or two new cows or buffaloes. Not our Gojri ones, where will they walk?

I firmly oppose resettlement policies. NOWHERE in the world has it been a process that led to justice. It divides up communities. And how do you resettle their ecosystem?
I think it is one more way to control things – our forest-dwelling people, our animals, and the land.

After the time I spent in the Deras, nestled between tall trees, it was unsettling to see Van Gujjar families working in their small wheat fields.

At one edge of the colony, we reach the house of Shamshad, also a VGTYS activist.

We had hundreds of animals in our care here before they cleared the forests.
And we used to move our homes from one place to another freely back then.
Now there's only a small part of the old forest left. We still use it even though the Junglaat threatens us.
When the trees were cleared for agricultural plots and families were forced to resettle here, we weren't even given a single plot of land!
Because, though we had lived here for generations, we had no papers to prove it ...

. We used to spend all our days playing deep in the forest as children!
A few of those old trees, like these banyans, are still around ...

As we walk around Shamshad's home, we meet his neighbour Fatima, busy rebuilding her home using the traditional mud brick method.
Those brick-and-cement rooms without windows are too hot in summer and too cold in winter. How will we survive??
But now it's hard to find the right type of grass and palm leaves to make our homes like we used to. They're all in the National Park area.

We find ways to continue some of our old practices even here. After many years of struggle, I now have some land in my name ...
Here, try this fruit. It is like an orange but completely different ... Someone brought it this morning from the forest.

Are there conflicts within the community between those who were here before and those who have been resettled here?
We stick together and help each other out. There are clearer differences between those who have remained in the forest Deras and those who have moved ...
Also we must remember that many families who were evicted from the National Park areas were NEVER even resettled ... Over 1,600 families were just thrown out.
They live on the river banks and the edges of villages, wherever they are allowed to.

Even the plots that were allotted to resettled families and to us are only on lease for twenty-five years. What happens after that?
JHILMIL JHEEL SANCTUARY
On our way out of Gendikhata, Ameer takes a longer route.
When the forests were cut down to make plots for the Resettlement Colony, all the animals ran towards the one area left uncut. So of course the State thought it profitable to turn that area into a wildlife park! Exploiting our ecosystem is an endless game for them.

I wanted to show you the Forest Department's most recent action.
This area is part of the Jhilmil Sanctuary, but in the name of afforestation, the Department has planted hundreds of Kanju Papri plants here, which is an extremely invasive species. It will slowly kill the native trees around and drain the soil. Then the birds and animals will vanish from here.
And then the Department will find some excuse to develop what they will wrongly call a 'wasteland'.
!!

We'll quickly stop by this settlement of Van Gujjar families. They lived in the area that is now the sanctuary!
We are still struggling to be resettled somewhere. We just get kicked around from one place to the other, trying to live close to the forests ...
In the old days, we used to move freely with our animals through these very lands.
I miss everything.

Ameer dropped me at the highway that night, and as I waited for my bus, my phone switched off. Suddenly, I felt unprepared for the world.
TRAINING COLLEGE
KORNER
RISHIKESH →
HARIDWAR ←
AIMS RISHIKESH ←
HORN PLEASE
Charging my phone at a small roadside tea stall with a make-shift plug point gave me some time to ponder.
But it felt impossible to make meaning of all that I had heard and seen, not just that day but over the past few months – of forced evictions, flawed conservation policies, control of land and the continuing legacy of the colonial Forest Department.

I thought about how Shamshad said that if they assert their rights to the forest through FRA too often, the Junglaat men destroy their crops and break their homes overnight ...
UTTARAKHAND TRAVELLER
That they break an elephant's tusks in the sanctuary area and blame Van Gujjars for it.
That the Junglaat threatens to plant more invasive species that destroy the Van Gujjars' land and that their cattle die grazing on.
'They don't want us here. Nor in the forest.
Where are we supposed to go??'

3. We are not your museum!

I was visiting my parents at their Dera near Nainital, but yes, you should plan to come back to Gendikhata!
Yes, so far I've met many of the men leading initiatives in the Resettlement Colonies, but I really want to hear your views on so much!
After months of planning, I finally return to Gendikhata to meet with Aamna and other women leaders at the Van Gujjar Resettlement Colonies.
DISASTER DRAWN

The train rides out to Uttarakhand, with its endless holy sites, are increasingly filled with Government advertisements glorifying development.
'Wellness' being a fast emerging keyword.
आज़ादी का अमृत काल!
उत्तराखण्ड सबसे आगे!
उत्तराखण्ड
INDIA'S NO.1 TOURISM

We meet at the highway where the road turns off into the Resettlement Colonies.
But instead of going down that route, Aamna speeds us off in another direction.
We're going to the Depot Dera first. We'll have to ride on the wrong side, but it's not far!

We walk past the Forest Office, which looks like a booming timber market, on to an unkempt area from where we spot the Dera at a distance.

One of my aunts is married into a family here, I haven't visited her for a while.
Most of us have some relative or the other all over the hills.
But now marriages between those still in the forests and those in Resettlement Colonies are less frequent – families feel that women will not be able to adjust between these two very different ways of living ...
Soon Aamna's aunt has us seated on the cot outside her home, and she gives us hot lunch and milky sweet Gojri tea.
I grew up in my uncle's house, which is closer to a town near Nainital. So unlike most Van Gujjar girls, I have studied well. Now I'm doing my BA and working with a local NGO to educate children here.

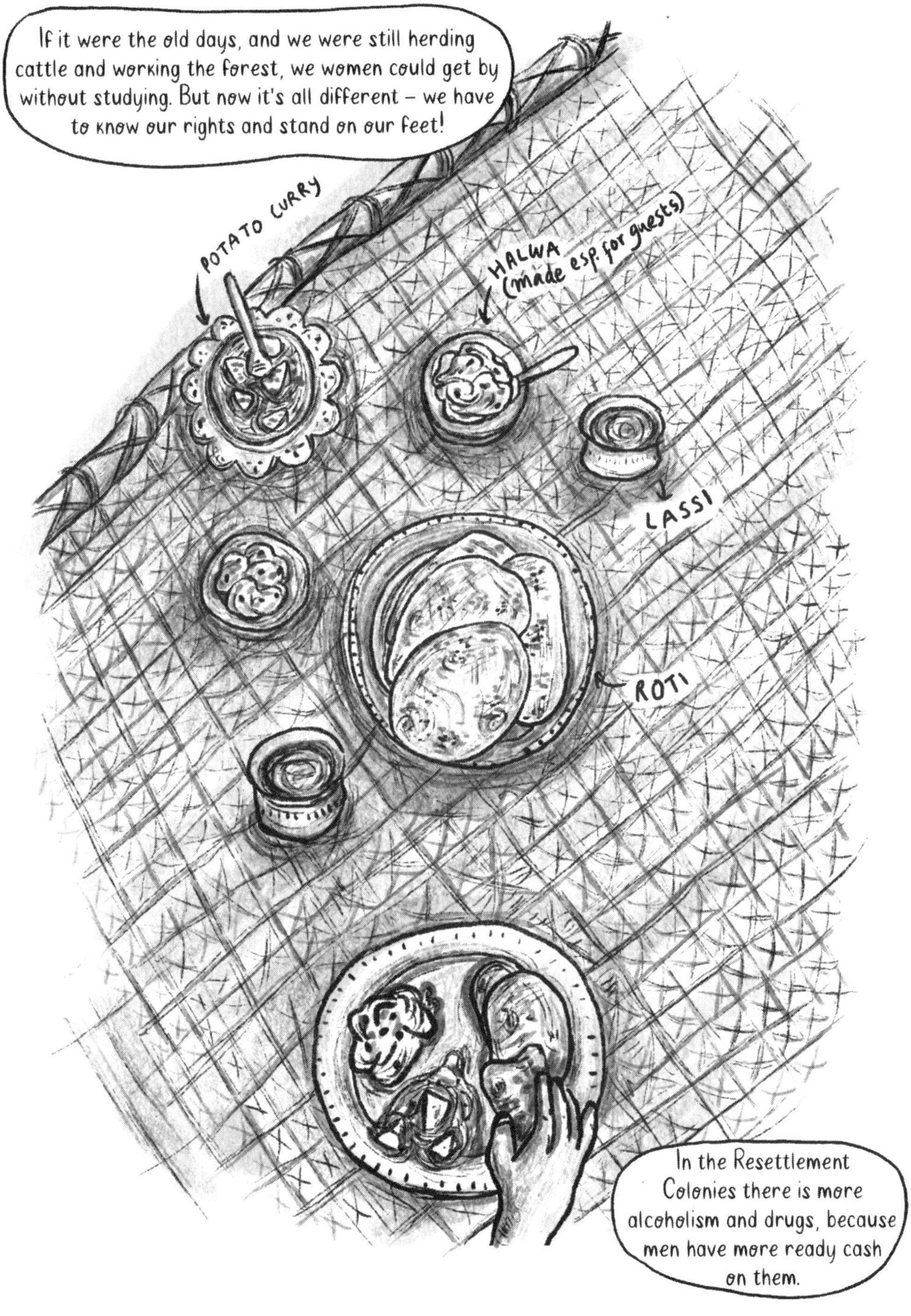
If it were the old days, and we were still herding cattle and working the forest, we women could get by without studying. But now it's all different – we have to know our rights and stand on our feet!
POTATO CURRY
HALWA (made esp. for guests)
LASSI
ROTI
In the Resettlement Colonies there is more alcoholism and drugs, because men have more ready cash on them.

And with that, the cases of violence against women have gone up drastically in our community! It's not unusual now to hear of a drunk man beating up his wife. There was even a rape in the community recently ...
Another BIG change that came with being settled into colonies near markets is that the groom's family now often asks for a dowry at the time of marriage.
Earlier on, it was the groom's family that used to give one buffalo to the bride's side. I think that was better.
In the forest Deras they still do that at least some of the time.

My brothers and sisters who grew up in the forest and weren't able to study are finding it hard now that lifestyles are shifting ...
!
Hey! That cow is eating up all the drying grain!
But there are often no jobs EVEN for those who have an education. Look around here - ALL the men have gone to do manual labour at construction sites in Haridwar, it is that season.

After chatting a while with Aamna's aunt, and helping her pack up the dried grain or what was left of it, we visited the family of one of the eldest women in that Dera. She'd had cancer for several years now, and after a series of fraudulent treatments from hospitals near and far, her family was keeping her safely at home in her last days.

At least when she's in her own home, with us around, she can breathe.

At home I've created a different routine for myself from what most women my age are expected to follow … I spend most of my day with my education projects.
We drive back in the chilly evening breeze to Aamna's home in the Resettlement Colony. She lives with her aunt and uncle, and their son.
My family and friends laugh at me for it. They tell me that once I'm married off I'll understand how things are supposed to be. But I'm never going to change!
You're finally back! I've fed the cows already, just go and quickly cook dinner for everyone.

It took me some time, but I do like it that Aamna has her job. Every morning she goes off on her scooty before I know it.
I couldn't even imagine doing that when I was growing up. We collected firewood, cooked, looked after the buffaloes. Even now my day goes into doing these things. After coming here I had to also learn how to farm.
I will do ANYTHING to leave this place. Right now, I'm learning computers.
He just keeps floating in his dream world all day, or else he's on his phone!

At night we walk to Aamna's elderly aunt's home, who, while the rest of her family sleeps, is full of stories for us.

And I remember that, earlier, if a man raised his hand to his wife or any woman, there used to be a 'penchi'.
The entire Dera would collect under the old Banyan tree, and that abusive man would be publicly humiliated for his actions. Even punished. He would be made to feel SO ashamed of what he had done.
I know that wasn't an ideal way, but nowadays we get stuck with telling the police, and all they want are bribes ... We are dependent on people who loot us and give us no justice.

Our elders speak endlessly of the old days. Of living amidst trees.
After all, this basti was born out of the death of a forest.
We have education, roads and electricity now, but neither enough land to feed ourselves, nor enough trees for fodder.
We are all stuck in between. So the younger generation dreams of leaving . . . for somewhere!
As we sleep under the stars, we can hear the foxes howl.

KUKRUKOOON!!!
Although agriculture has been forced on the Van Gujjars along with a more settled form of life, many have returned to also keeping buffaloes. For them, selling milk has once again become a primary source of income. The day, therefore, begins before the sun even rises. They gather fodder, collect milk and then deliver it collectively to the local 'lalas' who supply it to nearby towns and cities, but tend to give the Van Gujjars extremely low rates in return.
And as Aamna tells me, 'Historically, our community has had a strong link with the market, and towns around us have always needed our milk and ghee. But that relationship works when it's on our terms, not if we are looted and have no place for us to live or for our animals to walk!'

After a breakfast unlike one I've ever had, of smoky hot chulha roti with spicy chillies and sweet, thick buffalo milk cream, we hang out till Aamna needs to leave for her classes.
Mirchi
Roti with Ghee (lots)
Buffalo milk Malai (extra creamy)
It's so obvious to me that the relationship between nature and human settlements is maintained by those who go between these two with their animals - the pastoral communities.
So, if the Van Gujjars leave, suddenly everything goes out of balance here - the wild elephants and tigers lose their connection with people, then they grow scared and attack more often. And people in the nearby towns have no understanding of what to do with the forests.

The landscape and so much else is changing around us very fast. But you can't expect that we will stay the same.
Hasn't YOUR culture and family also changed? Why should WE stay exactly the same?
We are not your museum.

No matter what, we rely on each other. Look around here right now, the urad daal has to be harvested. My uncle will work on other people's farms and they will work on ours. And whoever has a tractor will help those who need it.

Slowly, women from our community need to be given leadership space in social movements.
We will become lawyers and pilots and educators. Some will leave and go far away but I know many will stay on here ...
I don't think 'oh I'm educated, let me take off from here'. No, I love my work of teaching children in the Resettlement Colony.

4. Taungya

Back in Delhi, long-time forest rights activist Roma tells me how she remembers walking with the Van Gujjars.

One summer, I trekked up with the Van Gujjars. Through forests, hills and highways. It was just after the Babri Masjid demolition in 1992, so you can imagine the tension felt by a Muslim nomadic community walking through hill villages and towns filled with temples!

Delhi Office,
All India Union of Forest Working People

But they will do ANYTHING for their buffaloes! Every day we were up at 4 a.m., gathering fodder and then walking.

I remember sitting in their camp up in Uttarkashi one evening and listening to the radio. To our shock, a Forest Department official was talking on the news about how Van Gujjars come up every year and cut down entire forests!
While all day actually we had been seeing THEIR labour, brought in all the way from Kashmir at that time, made to chop the forests across hillsides!
Then, every evening, those very officials would come down to the Dera and take away huge amounts of ghee and milk! It's still the same ...

It seems impossible for us to really grasp that forest land has been understood for centuries as common community resource. As something to protect collectively.
The colonial laws that continue today, from the Indian Forest Act onwards, are actually meant for trade. So it is very threatening for the Government-corporate nexus to imagine the masses of people living on forest land actually owning it! That's why they keep trying to find ways around the FRA.
FREE ALL POLITICAL PRISONERS
आज़ाद करो!
ELECTION WATCH 2024
Last year the Modi government passed the Forest Conservation Amendment Act, scrapping provisions for consent of local communities and other statutory requirements for forest clearance in vast areas. Estimates suggest that 30 million hectares of total forest area could be vested as community forest rights with the gram sabhas... the potential to secure the livelihoods of over 200 million people...

MINE
In Uttarakhand, which was earlier a part of Uttar Pradesh, the promised land redistribution barely took place. So land has remained in the grip of upper-caste landholders.

We went through records of how landowners put land parcels in the names of their animals, ancestors, even gods, all to prevent any redistribution to landless communities! And after Independence, forest land just went into the pockets of the same Forest Department.

Women Political Prisoners Meet
Delhi, 2023

Even the jails that you throw us into belong to us! They were built brick by brick by our hands. This whole country has been made by people who are being thrown off their land!
When I was in jail, I refused to eat the food they would give me. For five months I kept myself alive on fruits my visitors brought me and water!

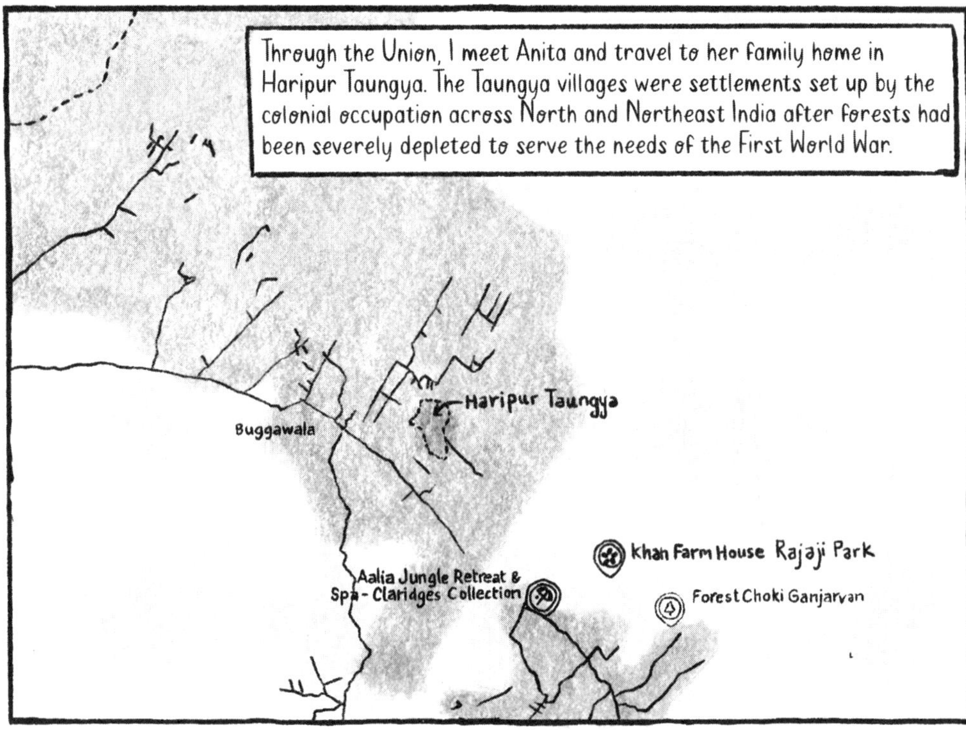
Through the Union, I meet Anita and travel to her family home in Haripur Taungya. The Taungya villages were settlements set up by the colonial occupation across North and Northeast India after forests had been severely depleted to serve the needs of the First World War.
Haripur Taungya
Buggawala
Khan Farm House
Rajaji Park
Aalia Jungle Retreat & Spa - Claridges Collection
Forest Choki Ganjarvan

Landless workers from across Hindu, Sikh and Muslim families were pushed into these settlements to reforest the landscape left bare, with the promise that, at the end of five years of work, they would be given land which would be in their names permanently. That is an ongoing struggle.

The meaning of Taungya is 'ubad-khaabad' zameen, land that can't be cultivated. It was completely unfertile, or else overgrown with bushes impossible to move through.
My great-grandparents and other landless and outcast labouring families came here in the 1930s. They dug the land, fed it, grew the trees and nurtured plantations all across this belt from UP to what is now Uttarakhand's foothills.
The land was painstakingly transformed into the forests everyone loves to see today. But the teak, poplar, eucalyptus trees were never meant for us. The Forest Department has had FULL authority over them. The land our homes stand on, it is still not in our name.

After the Indian government imposed its Forest Conservation Act in the 1980s, we suddenly became 'encroachers'. But if people are oppressed for centuries, I think they will always find a way to fight back!
Slowly, people like my father started to organise themselves against eviction. They had to sell their kitchen utensils to get some money to support this mobilisation ... But this is how collective struggles have always begun in our country.
If they hadn't organised the struggle, we would have been pushed out of here years ago! Haripur is full of broken roads, it has no drainage and no hospitals - but it is also the first Taungya village in this region with pukka houses! We have no fear of the forest authorities here.

As we walk down the broken streets, Anita talks about her village's now over thirty-year-long struggle for legal rights for land ownership, and their filing for Community Forest Rights under the FRA. We reach one end of the village that has a long boundary wall, behind which is the relatively swanky Forest Department Office. She says, 'Their eyes are always on us'.

I vow to God that I will do no such work by which the flora and fauna are hurt and I will catch or aid in catching any anti-social elements who bring such harm. Dear God, give me the power to accomplish this work.

– I, You and Us

Today, those old forests are a fantasy for us. We can never really use them. The jadi-booti from the forests gets collected by illegal contractors of the Forest Department. And we know they trade in wood.
Since there's no other work, people risk going in there to collect firewood to sell in bundles.
This is my grand-aunt's home. She was a Taungya plantation worker.

Bent over and barely mobile, Anita's 'Dadi' lights up when she sees us coming to sit with her.
What can I tell you?! We used to walk to work much before the sun was up. They kept us far from the trees.
We dug the hard rocks out. Cut off thorny bushes that tore our skin. Made tracks from the rivers to the fields. Planted thousands of saplings and watched over them.
Day and night.
Night and day.
Day and night.

We would protect the saplings from storms and droughts. As if they were our children.
As Taungya workers, we worked for five to seven years on one plantation, and as soon as the trees could stand on their own we were moved off.
While we worked, we could live in the basti. In the gap between the tree saplings, they allowed us to grow some food to live on. We grew gehun, urad daal, lauki.

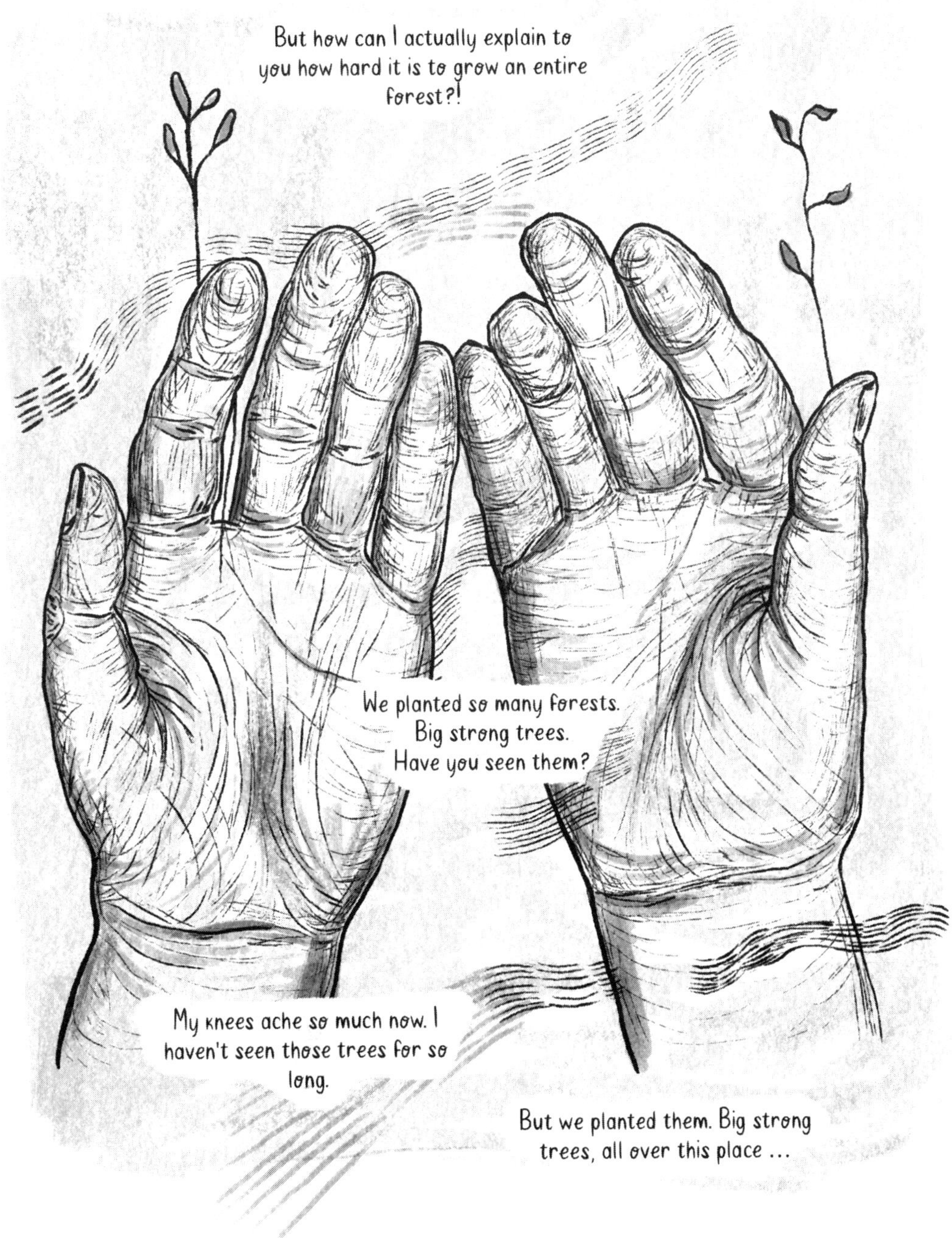
But how can I actually explain to you how hard it is to grow an entire forest?!
We planted so many forests. Big strong trees. Have you seen them?
My knees ache so much now. I haven't seen those trees for so long.
But we planted them. Big strong trees, all over this place ...

Our struggle for land rights, to feel like we belong to this country, is a long one.
That's why I've decided to become a lawyer, to be able to fight for our legal rights.
We also meet Anita's uncle who used to be a Forest Officer in the village.
I worked first as a watch guard for the Forest Department. Then I slowly rose up the ranks. It was my duty to watch over this village. The land. To make sure nobody is doing anything wrong ...

That is why the Forest Department is there. To protect the land!
But nobody should ask me questions about what I did during my time.
!
I always performed my duties well.
There is nothing more to say.

As the sun set, we left Haripur. As we drove, Anita and her brother continued to speak about the land and villages around us.
The Taungya system might have stopped, but gulamgiri has not. Governments use the Junglaat to keep threatening us. Hum unke kabze se nikalna chaahte hain. Hum bhi asal mein is desh ka hissa banana chahte hain. Uski hi toh ladaayi hai!

5. The Watchtower

At Aamna's wedding in the winter of 2022 at Gendikhata, her friend Teena comes speeding in on their two-wheeler with a big tin box.
Teena is the local expert on all things make-up and wedding dress-up.
But that's far from all –
I've been working to revive local Gojri craft forms. We have a long history of bead work and stitching. But it's slowly dying out as ways of living change and we get more things from markets ...

When families went up the mountains during the summer migration, they would keep these materials with them – beads, thread, needles, wool – or buy them along the way from traders.
Women would stitch and make things whenever they were done for the day with their animals. They would make special Gojri hats, little clothes for children, purses and beautiful jewellery!
Today, beads and thread are much more expensive, and the kind of glass beads we got earlier - very small, fine ones, are no longer available - the beads are bigger and don't have the same colours ...

For us, the patterns of these knitted works made by the older women using the Gojri method resemble walking through a wild forest ...
Over the following year, I learn more about the work Teena is doing, and get involved in trying to support it to make it a sustainable process - with all the ups and downs that come with such an endeavour.

Earlier I used to feel like our work has to have a place in some institution in Delhi or Dehradun. But when I tried to reach out to some of them, I got ZERO responses.
I now think that if anybody wants to learn about our culture and ways of living, they need to come here and see it.

We are shaping a new identity for ourselves. Even if we have been forcefully uprooted from the forests, we are still Van Gujjars. So then I ask myself, what does that mean to me?
I found these old photo frames, and I requested some of the eldest women to collect a few samples of their work ...

These days most women don't wear the kind of Gojri necklaces made with old coins or the bigger earrings, but many still wear some of bead jewellery they've made themselves.
I had to really promise that I would keep these pieces safe to get them here! We are all so proud of our old Gojri works.

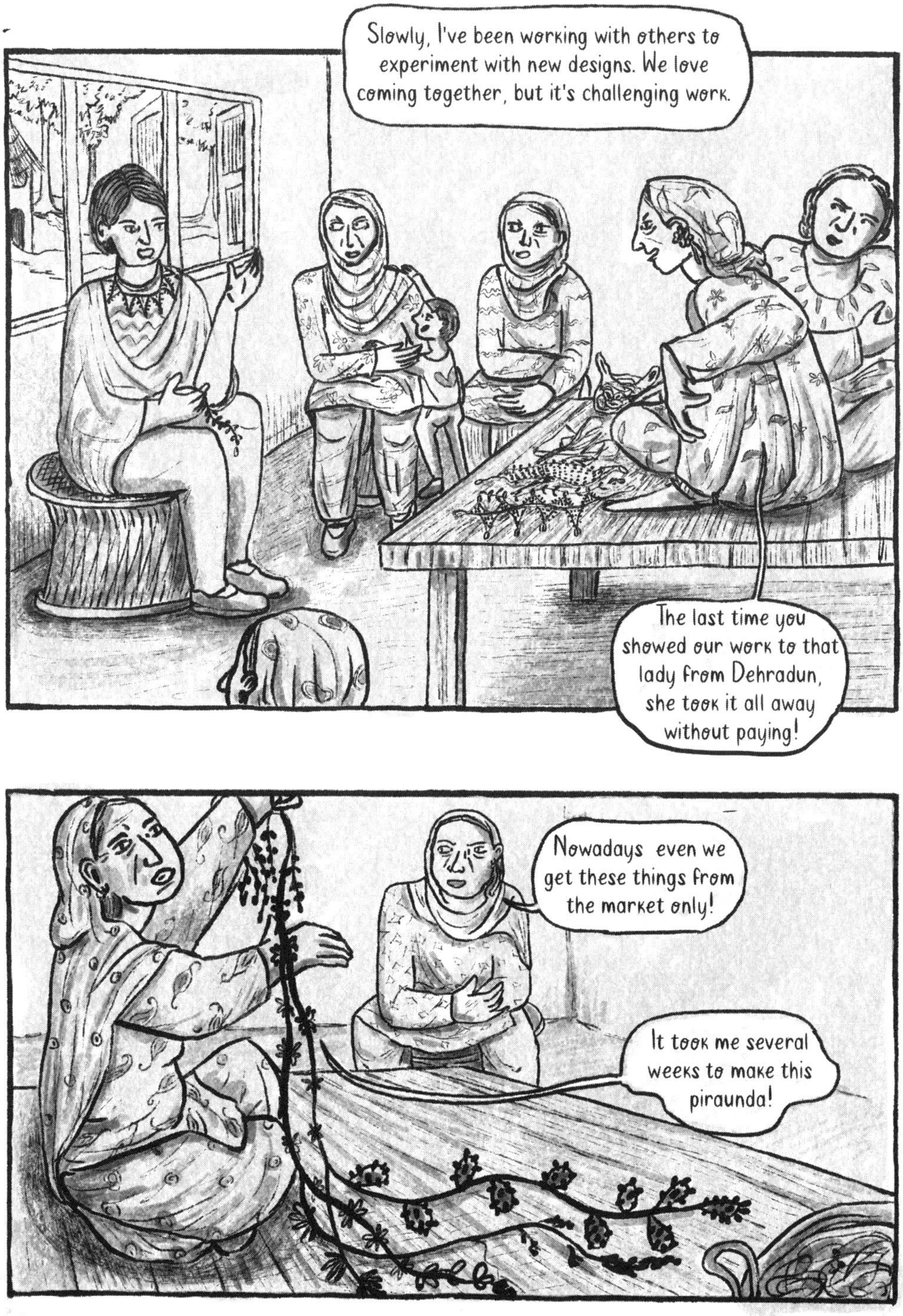
Slowly, I've been working with others to experiment with new designs. We love coming together, but it's challenging work.
The last time you showed our work to that lady from Dehradun, she took it all away without paying!
Nowadays even we get these things from the market only!
It took me several weeks to make this piraunda!

My community is also more accepting of differences than you'd imagine. I've always felt some level of acceptance here being a trans person, than when I travel in buses and trains or go to nearby cities like Haridwar.
My family and the other elders around may not really understand when I speak of the rights of trans people, but growing up they never let me feel like an outsider ...

I do still feel a sense of responsibility to talk about gender differences through our collective work, because there isn't enough understanding of it. And the young people want to know more.
There is also the risk of the many fraudulent ashrams in Uttarakhand that take in trans people, and they end up getting stuck serving elder leaders there. I want us to help each other out.

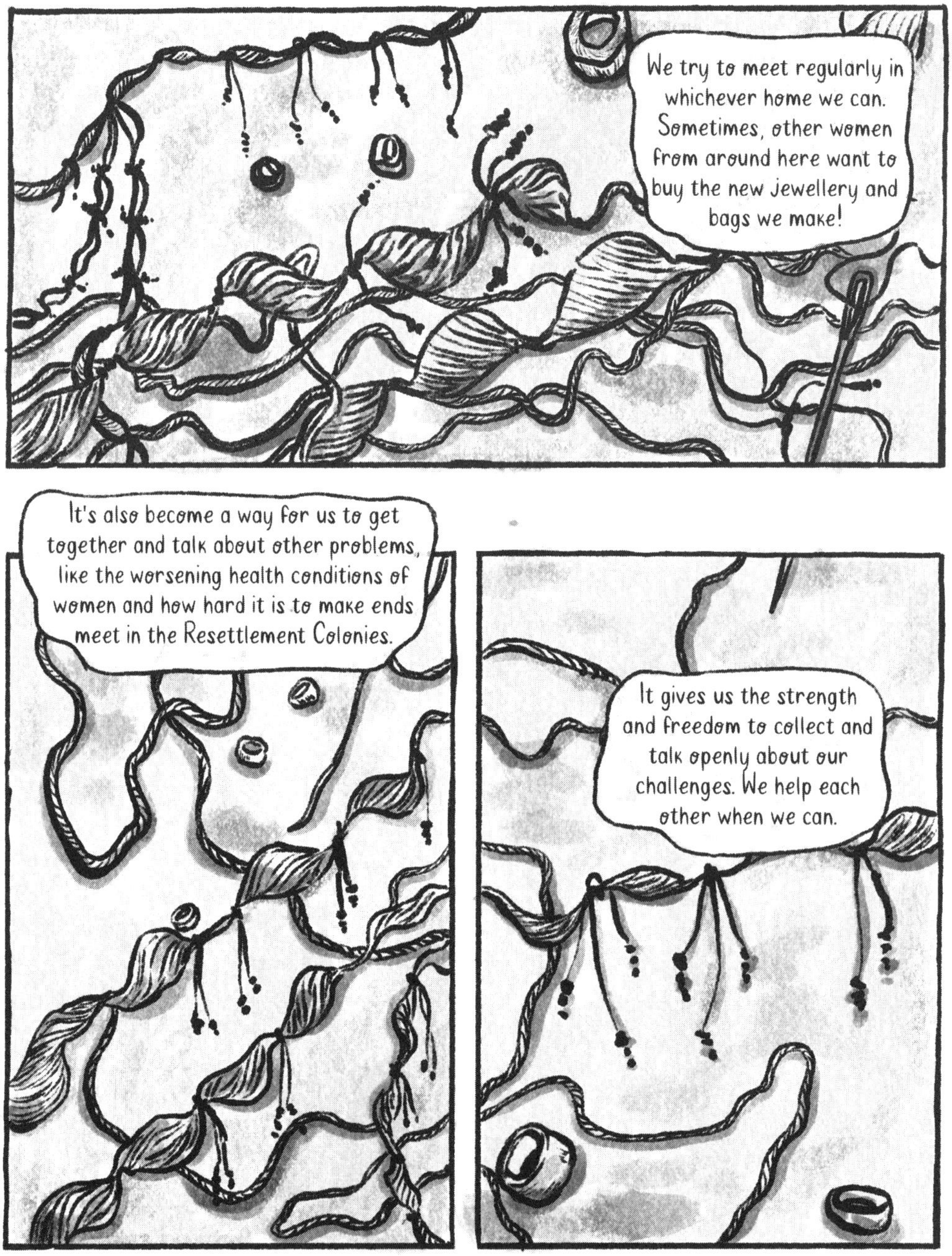
We try to meet regularly in whichever home we can. Sometimes, other women from around here want to buy the new jewellery and bags we make!
It's also become a way for us to get together and talk about other problems, like the worsening health conditions of women and how hard it is to make ends meet in the Resettlement Colonies.
It gives us the strength and freedom to collect and talk openly about our challenges. We help each other when we can.

Like when Najma's husband ran away, leaving her with her one-year-old baby, we were there for her.
Evey year, the unpredictable and heavy rains bring our homes crashing down. Forest fires burn all our fodder. How do you think we get back up?
Buttermilk
Mango pickle
Home-grown Daal & Rice
On one of our last days together in 2023, after a hearty meal, we take a long walk.

We're going to my favourite place ...

I feel like I can see the whole world from here! Over there are the last remaining homes of this old Van Gujjar Dera. The new Jhilmil Sanctuary for all you nature lovers. And then there's our Resettlement Colony ...
Forest Guard Watchtower, Jhilmil Jheel Sanctuary

When I come up here, I feel like we can do anything.
Let's stay till we see the deer come out.
The rickety tower shakes precariously as Teena, Najma, her daughter and I take in the grand expanse of green and blue.

UTTARAKHAND TRAVELLER

Acknowledgements

A heartfelt thank you to everyone who's been a part of this book—Noorjahan, Mustafa Chopra and both their families at Asarori, Ameer Hamza, Aftab, Shamshad, Aamna, Teena and their families, Roma, Ashok, Anita, Vipin and Sukalo Gond. Thank you to the Van Gujjar Tribal Yuva Sangathan and the All India Union of Forest Working People for bringing me into their ongoing work over the past few years, and for all the conversations along the way that have, gradually, become this book. I am very grateful to the many members of both the VGTYS and the AIUFWP who thoroughly reviewed drafts at many stages of the making of this book and also after it was brought together in its final form, prior to publishing. A big thank you to Ameer Hamza and Orijit Sen for writing their introductory notes without which the book would be incomplete. Thank you so much to Amita Baviskar and Suchitra Vijayan for their feedback and encouraging notes.

I am very grateful to Hemali and Ambar, and the entire team at A Suitable Agency, for believing in me from the get-go, and to Ambar for being there consistently for many essential conversations at various junctures in the creating process. Thank you very much to my editor, Ajitha, for giving the book a home, and to the entire team at Westland Books for bringing it into the world so caringly.

I'm very grateful for friends, family and mentors who've been so generous with their time, support and invaluable inputs at various points over the past few years—Zuha, Zanskar, Aditi, Lakshmi, Budhaditya, Amit, A.R. Vasavi, Simon, Mary, Kabir, Deepti and Nishant.